T0082604

# Roar of Freedom
## (inspiration, hope, love, and knowledge)

TONY BELL

authorHOUSE®

*AuthorHouse™*
*1663 Liberty Drive*
*Bloomington, IN 47403*
*www.authorhouse.com*
*Phone: 1 (800) 839-8640*

*© 2017 Tony Bell. All rights reserved.*

*No part of this book may be reproduced, stored in a retrieval system, or transmitted by any means without the written permission of the author.*

*Published by AuthorHouse 04/12/2017*

*ISBN: 978-1-5246-8844-8 (sc)*
*ISBN: 978-1-5246-8843-1 (e)*

*Print information available on the last page.*

*Any people depicted in stock imagery provided by Thinkstock are models, and such images are being used for illustrative purposes only. Certain stock imagery © Thinkstock.*

*This book is printed on acid-free paper.*

*Because of the dynamic nature of the Internet, any web addresses or links contained in this book may have changed since publication and may no longer be valid. The views expressed in this work are solely those of the author and do not necessarily reflect the views of the publisher, and the publisher hereby disclaims any responsibility for them.*

*Inspirational*

# *"Power"*

If the love the share with another is real-
love has the power to breath life into another another human being-
love is a powerful thing

# "Awaken"

Everyday you awaken is another chance for you to create the life you always wish you had-

# "Believe"

Believe in yourself-
turn adversity into ambition

# "Strength"

Stay strong mentally and you will survive physically-

# *"Unity"*

When the mind-the body-the spirit becomes one you ascend as a man or woman you become more-you become knowledge-wisdom-courage-inspiration

# "*Growth*"

Knowledge is the soil needed to replenish our earth (human beings)

# "Paths"

The beauty of the path you take is not to break you- but to simply teach you personal growth so you can grow into the person you're meant to be-

# *"Colors"*

One color alone is just a color- many colors together is art-

# *"Courage"*

Having the courage to push forward when the obstacle you're pushing is almost immovable- look inside yourself- find the courage to keep pushing forward-

# "Mirror"

The reflection which reflects back is the
image of ourselves and who we are-

# "Illusion"

The illusion of being broken constantly presents itself-
but how can you be broken when you can clearly see yourself-

# "Hope"

There's a light of hope in all of us- that light is your inner strength-
that inner strength is your free will to decide who you are who you
want to be in life-

# "Natures Beauty"

There's beauty in nature-
there's beauty in life-
we are nature-
we are life-
until you understand the connection between life and nature
you will never understand how truly beautiful our world is-

*Love poems*

# "Completion"

Love is when 2 incomplete halves come
together to make 1 complete whole-

# "Your Beauty"

Your beauty reminds me of a field of freshly bloomed roses-
The softness of your skin-
the silkiness of your lips-
the glistening of your gorgeous eyes-
the way your hair sways back and forth into the wind-
only an angel can compare to your beauty-
Aphrodite herself looked upon you and declared you were going to
be her image-
never again will such beauty be gazed upon again-

# "Love"

Love is like a flower- you must nurture it-
you must protect it-
you have to shower it with understanding-compassion-respect-
you have to fertilize it with trust-loyalty-eqaulness-
love is like a flower-you must cherish it-
love is like a flower-you have to sow a healthy seed and well mannered soil-
love is like a flower- treat it and it will never stop growing-

## "*Alive*"

Even though I'm alive-
deep inside I feel like I've died-I've never given up-
everytime I've been knocked down I've picked myself up-
I't isn't easy having the heart of a lion-
on the outside I'm smiling-
on the inside I'm crying-
inside feel as if I'm dying-
asking myself why times so trying-
but I promise I'm keep fighting-
to live the life I deserve to live- only way I stop if my heart give-
I live by a warriors creed-
I'll never let life destroy me-

# "The End"

The end is near-
the fear is near-
the teers roll down my face into into my my ears-
life rips at me like a pair of torn jeans-
my heart is busting at the seams-
It seems to be a bad dream-a bad dream
I can't wake up from-a bad dream
with no end- I lay under the fan-
this decision I'm not ready to take-but if I have to I will-

# "Till it end"

I await laying sleepless and confused
waiting till it end-the storm that's brewing outside my window-
the rain pouring like teers of my balcony door-
the thunder shaking and rattling the pictures on my wall-
as I lay under my blanket and cuddled and cradled-
as I drift into a deep sleep wondering will I awaken
to see the sun shining one more day-the storm is gone-

*Dedicated to my mom*

# "Mom"

Mom I miss you-
I miss the days I can't hug and kiss you-
all the bad times-
all the times
you were kind-
all the good days-
all your amazing ways-
I can't forget all the times
we had- sometimes
I just fall in my thoughts and get sad-
you were an amazing woman-all the things you showed me-
you're my everything-my every fiber-my every being-
love you and miss you my queen- dedicated to my mom (Mary Bell)

*Soft poetry*

# "Unseen"

In our darkest hour-our unseen angels are watching over us-in our
moments of despair-
our guardians are there-the love we have for our lost ones-
it never leaves just lives inside our heart-
the memories of our beloved ones keep us close-
our success and happiness gives them peace-their in our hearts forever-
therefore they never truly leave-

# *"No turning back"*

I've made it through the storm and now I'm here-I've put in the work now I can't turn back-
I've been waiting on this moment fighting for stability for my kids and my wife-
that's my motivation-that's my ambition-
they reason I can't turn back-

## *"Imperfection"*

We live in a imperfect world-with imperfect human beings
-life isn't about what you think it is-but rather what you make it-
success is built on determination-
motivation is built on ambition-
change is built on willingness to change-in the face of adversity
be that one person who's willing to fight for change-
fight for love-and fight for success-

# "Undisclosed"

Leaving my feelings exposed-everyday I feel more and more chosen-
so many thoughts it gets overwhelming-
if you can relate let me in-trying to maintain in this world of sin-
so much buried in the closet-
life keep testing me-
lord keep blessing me-
save work for idol hands -heart heavy-
knees shaky-
I can barely stand-
success I'm fighting to get it- fighting to make it-
I just want to influence my people to do better-
if you know better we have to do better-

# "Rebirth"

Trying to stay focused-
trying to keep myself in a positive position-
for the troubled minds I want you to listen-
regardless of the things you've done-
don't mean your life is over just keep going-
there's such thing as rebirth-
despite your past-
despite the hurt-
don't give up keep pushing forward-
you have to take it-
you have to keep fighting if you want to make it-

# "Hands of time"

If I could turn back the hands of time-
I would have done a lot of things different-
I would have thought twice about some of the things I've done-
I would have created a future for myself a long time ago-
I would have showed human beings more love-
more tenderness-more understanding-
I would have appreciated my mom more before she went above-
if I could turn back the hands of time-

# "The walk"

The walk I walk is along one-
the journey is challenging-
the obstacles are defining-
yet I remain strong in my walk-
I remain sincere in the way I talk-
I grasp the hardships of overcoming trial and tribulation-
who am i? I am the man who walks strong-
I am the man who walks alone-
I am the man who stays strong-

# "Divine"

I've walked a hard line-
I've paid my dues with time-
I was young-I was weak-
I was out my mind-
after what I've been through I'm destined to be divine-
don't ever let life make you-
don't ever let life break you-
don't ever let life take you –
be the keeper of your own future-
give a little effort it'll make a big difference-
I was born to be great-
I won't expect anything less-

# *"Different"*

People fear what they don't understand-
people fear what they can't handle-
People fear what's different-
people fear the change necessary in life-
people fear the difference changing your mentality to have a healthy life-
people don't understand how lost you'll be without difference-

# "Pain"

Pain is inevitable in this life-
pain is needed to grow in this life-
pain is needed to mold you into the warrior you need to become
in this life-
pain is needed to appreciate the good that comes in your life-
pain is needed for survival-
pain is needed to become stronger-
pain is life-
pain guides-i
n the end pain helps us succeed-

# "Raise up"

There's comes a time when you have to stand up-
if you believe in change you can't give up-
sometimes you have to fight for what's right-
In the midst of darkness you have to be the light-
you want a better life you're going to have to fight-
life is hard but you have to keep your hands up-
keep pushing forward for a better future-
the future is depending on us-the world needs us-

# "Reincarnation"

To be reincarnated is to be reborn-
to be given a second chance at life-
rebirth of yourself but in a different perspective-
reincarnation is when your old self dies and a new being is born
inside your old body-
reincarnation is to awaken and see the beauty in everything you
took for granted-
reincarnation is to be mentally reborn-
reincarnation is be spiritually rejuvenated-
reincarnation is to be emotionally acceptable-
dependable-and strong within yourself-

*Loetry*
*(life/poetry)*

# "Reason"

People come in your life for a reason
-even if it's meant for them to only stay for a season-
everybody-
every situation is a lesson-
you heart broken but you still breathing so count your blessings-
in a world of hate you constantly being tested-
tired and exhausted from not being able to rest-
realising at times my good heart trying to escape my chest-
I find it sad how human beings treat the opposite flesh-
I find it sad you have so much talent but scared to give your best-
you have right to choose the path you take-
you have an obligation to give everything you need to give to make it-

# "Change"

It's 2017 time for change-
each and every one has the power to change things-
this world have my people thinking it's ok to hate each other-
only way for us to overcome opposition is to love each other-men
and women suffering without clothes or covers-
I sit countless hours wondering-pondering-
the shots I hear in the sky are thundering-
I keep my head up looking to the clouds-
the biggest problems we face is racism and diversity-
we have to come together to overcome this adversity-
even if I have to stand alone-ill stand strong-

# "Knowledge"

Give me an ear listen to this knowledge-
music, books, and history keeps our minds polished-
don't be afraid to exploit your potential-in this world it's essential-
in this life knowledge is needed for personal growth-
knowledge is needed for progression and success-
knowledge is beneficial for our future-
I don't my nephew and kids to go through what I been through-when this generation is gone-
who's going to teach our kids how to be strong-

# "Pain" Pt 2

This pain I feel in my bones-somedays It's hard to walk but I get up
and moving on-
if you don't feel pain how you know you alive-
I fight through the pain and keep striding-
tossing and turning at night being awakened by the sensation of being
eaten alive-
somedays feel as if I can't function-
life keeps hitting me with low blows-
but I get up and keep punching-
I'll never give up that's a fact-
to never surrender -never give up-that's my pact-

# "Roar in the clouds"

When you feeling down-
take a sec to look at the clouds-
you blessed to see another day-
all these hardships I wouldn't have it any other way-
when it's dark I dance in the rain-
let the rain wash away all my pain-
I'm strained-
can't be mad after everything I've gained-
there's always light after rain-
all I ask is for you to stay strong-
each and every one has the ability to carry on-

# *"Lost"*

Lost in my mind-
lost in time-
lost in life-
I don't want to fight-
fighting to hold to this little bit of light-
losing sight-
losing sight of what's right-my mind screaming-
finding it hard to dream-feel like I don't belong in this realm-
feel as if I'm over whelmed-
but I look inside myself and remember my path-
can't give up have to stick to this path-

Printed in the United States
By Bookmasters